PORTRAIT SERIES — PS13

Northamptonshire Narrow Gauge Railways in the 1960s

Sydney A. Leleux

Motor Rail 'Simplex' 8731 of 1941 locomotive and wagons in the quarry of Earls Barton Silica Sand Co. Ltd, 14th July, 1965.

THE OAKWOOD PRESS

Printed by© 2021 Sydney Leleux
First Published in the United Kingdom, 2021
The Oakwood Press
54-58 Mill Square, Catrine, KA5 6RD
www.stenlake.co.uk

ISBN 978-0-85361-752-5

Printed by
Claro Print,
Office 26, 27, 1 Spiersbridge Way,
Thornliebank,
Glasgow G46 8NG

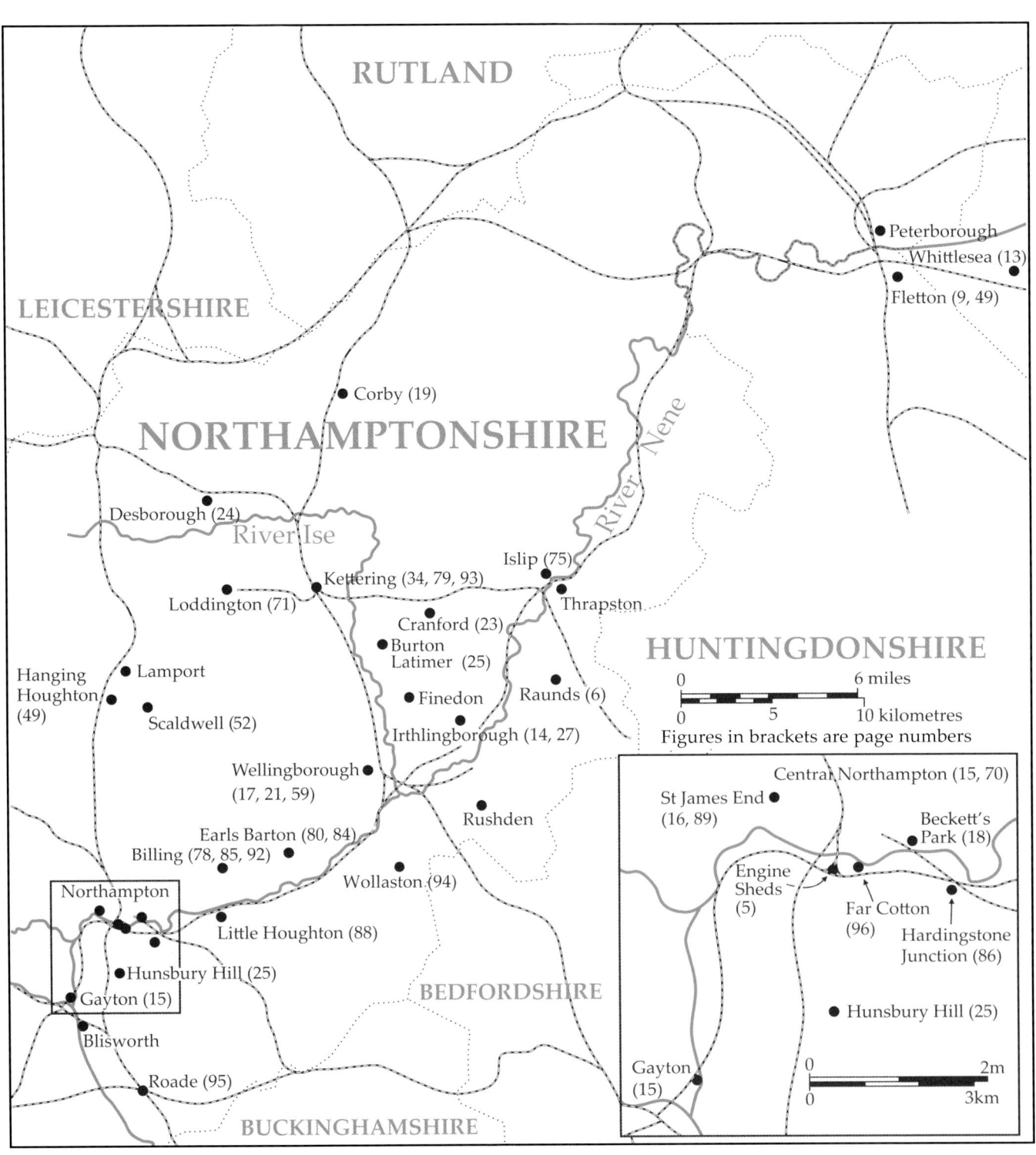

Contents

Location	Railway Use	Gauge(s)	Page
Billing	Pleasure railway	2 ft	78
	Sand & gravel	2 ft	85
	Sewage	2 ft	92
Burton Latimer	Gannister	2 ft	25
Corby	Basic slag fertilizer	2 ft	19
Cranford	Gannister	2 ft	23
Desborough	Ironstone	2 ft	24
Earls Barton	Sand & gravel	2 ft	1, 84
	Silica	2 ft	80
Finedon	Sewage	2 ft	93
Fletton	Brickworks	2 ft 6 in. & 2 ft 11 in.	9, 49
Gayton	Clay pit	2 ft	15
Hanging Houghton	Ironstone	3 ft	49
Hunsbury Hill	Ironstone	3 ft 8 in.	25
Irthlingborough	Cement	2 ft	14
	Ironstone mine	3 ft	27
Islip	Ironstone	3 ft	75
Kettering	Council	2 ft	93
	Ironstone	3 ft	34
	Pleasure railway	2 ft	79
Little Houghton	Sand & gravel	2 ft	88
Loddington	Ironstone	metre	71
Northampton	Ash disposal	2 ft 10¼ in. & 3 ft	5
	Contractors	Monorail	15
	Fellmongering	2 ft	18
	Pleasure railways	7¼ in. & 9½ /10¼ in.	70
	Sand & gravel	2 ft	86, 89
	Timber	1 ft 6 in.	96
Raunds	Brickworks	2 ft	6
Roade	Sewage	Monorail	95
Scaldwell	Ironstone	3 ft	52
Wellingborough	Contractors	2 ft	17
	Prefabricated building panels	2 ft, 3 ft & 5 ft	21
	Ironstone	metre	59
Whittlesea	Brickworks	2 ft & 3 ft	13
Wollaston	Sewage	Monorail	94

Introduction

My parents moved from Guildford, Surrey, to Northampton in the summer of 1955 when I was just 16. Northampton remained my home until my wife and I moved to West Yorkshire in the summer of 1966, although I periodically visited the town to see my parents until they died some twenty years later. In 1955 I had been a railway enthusiast for a long time, but mainly main line, although I had a relatively new and growing interest in narrow gauge, but I knew very little about industrial railways as such.

With the mass of information now readily available, it is worth pointing out how little there was generally available back then. There had been a few industrial railway enthusiasts before the Second World War, but they were the exception. The Birmingham Locomotive Club – Industrial Locomotive Information Section (phew! – BLC-ILIS for short), now the Industrial Railway Society, had been founded in 1949. The Narrow Gauge Railway Society, founded in 1951, also covered industrial lines. By 1959 I had learned of the existence, and joined, both societies. With the amount of steam then existing, even on the narrow gauge, non-steam lines tended to take second place, and some people shrugged off narrow gauge petrol or diesel locomotives as 'lawnmowers'!

My first discoveries were by chance, but later I was greatly assisted by two publications. In October 1959 I went as a new student to King's College, Strand, London, and soon visited Foyle's bookshop to look for material for my course. While there I made a detour to the railway section, and found a copy of the recently published *Ironstone Railways & Tramways of the Midlands* by Eric Tonks. I bought a copy and it led me to discover a number of railways close to my home. Indeed, protected in a polythene bag, it accompanied me on many subsequent railway explorations. Then in 1960 the BLC-ILIS published *Pocket Book D Industrial Locomotives of Eastern England* which included Northamptonshire. That gave me many more places to visit. With 102 A6 pages covering eight counties it shows how little was then known, when compared to the IRS book *Industrial Locomotives of Buckinghamshire Bedfordshire & Northamptonshire* published in 2001 which has 416 A5 pages (excluding illustrations) for just three counties.

Visiting industrial premises to see its railway was generally quite easy. Very occasionally I would write for permission, but usually I just turned up at the works office and asked to see the manager. Having explained my desire to see and photograph their railway, permission was almost invariably given, typically in terms 'Help yourself, watch where you go, and let us know when you leave.' Health and Safety was not an issue, common sense was assumed! If the shed or quarry was remote from the office then I might just walk in. Staff at all levels were often intrigued by my interest in 'their' railway.

For a time I worked for some accountants, many of whose clients were co-operative retail societies. In those days virtually every town and many villages had its own independent Co-op, each requiring an audit every six months before declaring its members' dividend (payment based on each member's purchases in the preceding half year). We usually travelled to the clients by bus or in the boss' car, but occasionally we went by train. Some Co-op offices had an industrial railway nearby, which I could visit in my lunch hour, occasionally even borrowing a bicycle from the office staff so I could have longer on site.

I bought my first 35 mm camera in December 1959, using earnings from work as a temporary Christmas postman. I soon discovered that cassettes could be refilled, first using prepared 36 exposure lengths, then cutting 5 m lengths to size, then even more economically buying 17 m lengths. Coupled with developing films at home and postponing printing meant that the cost of black and white photography was quite low. This was in complete contrast to colour slides, which, in my terms as a student, cost money, even though processing was included. The other problem was the low speed of colour film. I was used to Ilford FP3 at 200ASA, and Kodachrome (10ASA) or the slightly cheaper Agfacolour (24ASA) could be limiting when visiting a railway, particularly on a dull winter day. Not infrequently I even changed from colour to black and white, or vice versa, part way through a film, making a careful note how many exposures had been taken and taking great care not to wind the leading tongue back into the cassette when doing so. Once I bought a Ferrania Colour film and its home processing kit, which was an interesting experience. Some of the photographs at Scaldwell Quarries, including the cover, were taken using this film. Having watched a locomotive leave the 'curve' – succession of straights in fact – at Kettering's Quarry, jolting sideways at each rail joint, I bought an 8mm cine camera, and thereafter tended to use cine for colour and movement, and black and white for the rest, which is why there are so few colour shots in the book.

In addition to notes made on my visits, information has mainly been obtained from the publications mentioned above: Tonks' book and the BLC-ILIS and IRS books covering Northamptonshire.

Northampton Engine Sheds

Most British steam locomotives burnt coal, and the incombustible ash fell into an ash pan beneath the firebox. At the end of a spell of duty the ash pan had to be emptied, usually by raking the ash into a pit. In addition, clinker – ash fused into lumps by the heat of the fire – had to be shovelled out of the firebox and sometimes the remains of the fire was emptied out as well. Periodically labourers would shovel the piles of ash, clinker and unburnt fuel into wagons for disposal, a labour intensive operation.

In 1931 the London Midland & Scottish Railway began a programme of engine shed modernization, which reached Northampton Engine Sheds (SP747596) in 1938. The shed was located in the triangle of tracks half a mile south of Castle Station. The work included a new turntable, shed roof, water softener and probably the ferro-concrete ash disposal plant. Two old bullhead rails were laid on their side along the floor of the pit and concreted in, forming a 34¼ in. gauge railway. Small hopper wagons, 33¼ in. long, 47 in. wide and about 26 in. deep, running on 14½ in. diameter disc wheels, or 12 in. diameter 6-spoke wheels, on 35 in. wheelbase, could be positioned directly under the ash pan and carried the ash at one end of the pit where they could be emptied into a skip bucket. This lifted the ash up to discharge into a hopper for storage and later loading a wagon.

A pair of rails were laid upright beside the pit, with their outer faces 36 in. apart. The ground outside the rails was then concreted to within an inch of the top of the rails, and the ground between them was concreted flush with the top of the rails, forming a good surface from which to shovel any spillage. Some hopper wagons ran on the railway beside the pit, but because there was no flange way due to the concrete the wheels were turned round so that their flanges bore against the outer faces of the rails. These wagons could be pushed to empty into the same skip which served the pit.

About twenty LMS sheds had these ash pit railways with outside flanged wheels, so the 3 ft 5½ in. gauge railway with outside flanged wheels at Swanscombe Cement Works, Kent (converted to standard gauge in 1928) was not unique as is often supposed.

The lower photograph, taken on 30th October, 1965, shows a hopper wagon on the pit railway, with the end of the track of the outside line visible on the right. The one above shows two hopper wagons with their wheels reversed. There were seven wagons on site.

Raunds Manor Brickworks

Smith & Son (Raunds) Ltd operated Raunds Manor Brickworks half a mile east of the town (TL003725). A railway brought clay from the pit to the works. Originally operated by a steel cable from a stationary engine, by the time I first visited in June 1964 it had been replaced largely by a tractor and trailer, unless the weather was very wet when the tractor could not be used. Periodically damaged unfired bricks were collected and taken back to the clay input mill, where they were ground down for reuse. The upper photograph, taken on 21st July, 1964, shows the unloading area and clay stock pile, with the railway covered over for the tractor.

Locomotive haulage was introduced in 1934 with a second-hand Orenstein & Koppel diesel, sold after a new petrol Lister, 7280, came in 1936. This was found abandoned in a shed where bricks were stacked to dry before firing, lower photograph 22nd July, 1964.

The locomotive in use was a more modern Lister, 36743 of 1951, originally petrol but converted to diesel in 1962, shown after it had been pushed out of its shed, on 21st December, 1965. The shed was the body of a Southern Railway van, with extra doors cut in the end.

On my first visit, 23rd June, 1964, it was stored beside the William Foster, Lincoln, overtype steam engine, No. 14736, which used to power the works. It was kept as standby but had not been used for probably twenty years.

An unusual Ruston Hornsby diesel, 193984 of 1939, with a water tank instead of a radiator, stood in the long grass in the yard, 22nd July, 1964, spare to the newer Lister. It had a Hunslet Exhaust Gas Conditioner and Spark Arrester behind the cab, no doubt a relic of earlier employment elsewhere. Empty steel skips stood on the main line behind, with bodies tipped to avoid filling with rain water.

Above: In the bushes, derelict, was a hopper wagon, 25th June, 1964, with a home-made wooden body on a skip underframe, one of two used before steel skips were introduced.

Left: Off the rails in the works was a mobile air compressor, 23rd June, 1965, possibly for powering pneumatic spades if they were used in the clay pit.

London Brick Co., Fletton

Strictly, the brickworks which follow should not be included, as Fletton, south of Peterborough, was just over the county boundary in Huntingdonshire, and Whittlesea a bit further east was in Cambridgeshire, but the systems to be described are too close and interesting to ignore.

My cycling route to the Norfolk Broads for a sailing holiday was through Peterborough, about 40 miles from Northampton, and on 25th March, 1960 I took the opportunity to see a working 2 ft 11 in. gauge Sentinel steam locomotive in the London Brick Co.'s Hicks Works in Fletton, on the southern outskirts of the city. (TL191962)

Above and top: Sentinel 7701 of 1929 had a vertical boiler in the cab, supplying high pressure superheated steam to a high speed engine under the front bonnet. A chain drive took power from the gearbox to the rear axle, and on the other side another chain coupled the axles together. It was low built, to fit under bridges on its route between No. 1 & No. 2 works, and was used to haul trains of 'green' (unfired) bricks from the brick-making plant to the kiln.

Left: The low-slung wagons each carried two trolleys stacked with unfired bricks, and had roofs to keep them dry.

Nearby, crossing the East Coast Main Line on a bridge, was a 2 ft 6 in. gauge railway having a continuous cable between the rails to haul wagons individually clipped to it. Closely spaced inclined pulleys guided the cable round curves.

On the far side of the main line was another 2 ft 11 in. gauge railway serving New Peterborough Works (TL195958). A huge Simplex stood at the head of a train, but for some reason I ignored it for 91, another Simplex, 7998 of 1947. Maybe I was attracted by its spring buffers.

When I turned round, the huge Simplex, 9910 of 1942 (*above*), had gone, but Rob Pearman has provided a photograph. It was in rather better condition when I saw it, with a full set of bonnet covers. It was 65hp, weighing 9 tons, had a red body with black frames, and was the only example of its type in the UK.

Three years later, 28th October, 1963, I was again in Peterborough and took the opportunity to look at yet another cable operated railway in Fletton on the west side of the A15 (TL188962). The photograph (*left*) clearly shows the double track line serving the clay pit (about ¾ mile away to the south-west) with the wagons spaced along it. At the works the tracks branched to serve at least two brick-making plants.

Wagons entered the plant at first floor level, being hauled up a ramp well provided with hinged traps to catch the axles of any loaded wagon which started to run backwards down the gradient. There was presumably a mechanism inside the building not only to tip the wagons but to reverse them down the other track.

For obvious reasons a continuous haulage cable cannot go across points. On the approach to a junction the track was raised by a foot or so, and at the summit there was a vertical pulley (to lead the cable underground) in a strong metal housing. When the gripper on a wagon reached the housing, the housing forced the gripper open so releasing the cable, enabling the wagon to run free down the sloping track, across any points and crossings, until the gripper encountered another housing containing a pulley guiding the cable up from underground. This housing opened the gripper and on leaving the housing the gripper again fastened itself on the cable. The photograph shows the ramp for a detaching point just behind the wagon, which is about to attach itself to the cable having just run across the junction under its own momentum.

Whittlesea Central Brick Co.

Continuing my journey to the Broads, 25th March, 1960, I came to a bridge over the railway serving Whittlesea Central Brick Co. No. 1 Works (TL24248973). Here there was a 2 ft gauge double track incline out of the clay pit, with ordinary V-skips to carry clay to the works. Each skip body had a short steel upright centrally at each end, with a V slot cut into the top of the upright. The links of the continuous haulage chain fitted into the slot, thus gripping the wagon (*right*). At the bottom of the incline, on the clay pit floor, a shed covered the return wheel at the end of the chain haulage, and the men who pushed individual loaded wagons on to the chain and the empties away from it. A double track, locomotive worked line, took the wagons to the working face, where a tall vertical bucket excavator cut the clay and filled them. On 29th October, 1963 No. 2 Works (TL240972) had a 3 ft gauge Ruston Hornsby, 248360, hauling green unfired bricks, again on covered wagons (*below*).

Cement works, Irthlingborough

British Portland Cement Manufacturers once had a works in Irthlingborough (SP938700), closed in 1928 but used as a storage depot until 1950, when it was abandoned. When I visited the site on 19th November, 1964, having seen it marked on an old 25 in. OS map in the Co-op offices, it was, or had been, a Civil Defence training ground. The former 2 ft gauge shed for the quarry locomotives still stood, complete with its water tank over the door. The brick building was 35 ft long by 19 ft wide, with a pit at the door end only (*below*).

When the works had been in operation the first locomotive had been a rare product of the Glasgow Railway Engineering Co. in 1897 set up by the well known locomotive designer Dugald Drummond and scrapped around 1941. It was very similar to Kerr Stuart 721 of 1901 preserved in the Narrow Gauge Museum, Tywyn.

Drawing of Drummond's locomotive by G.Alliez 2008A, *Author's collection*

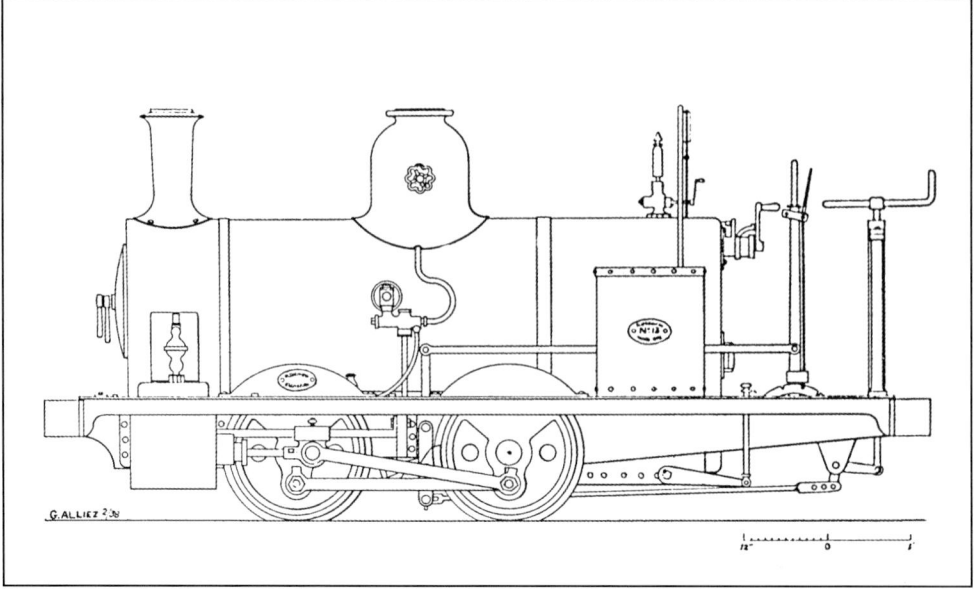

Gayton clay pit

British Waterways had a site near Gayton Wharf, Blisworth, now marked on the OS map as a marina (SP721554). Then it was a sunken overgrown area, partially flooded, with a single 2 ft gauge track laid in light 14lb/yard rail running from a tiny wharf on the canal bank west towards the current working area. Several lengths of track, and a pair of points, were scattered around the site. Apparently it had once been a brickyard, then became a source of clay for stopping leaks in the canal. There were two skip frames, one with inside frames and the other the more common outside frames, designed to carry an end tipping body mounted transversely across the frame. Note the very light rails, concreted in and turned up at the end to prevent a wagon going into the canal, with two maintenance boats, September 1962. I did not enter the swampy area to photograph the wagons closely!

Contractors' Monorails in Northampton

In the late 1940s Road Machines (Drayton) Ltd developed a monorail system which was quite popular before small dumper trucks became ubiquitous on construction sites. The first one I saw was on a building site in Lower Harding Street, Northampton in June 1961, being used by Bernard Sunley & Sons. This photograph shows the initial design of monorail unit, with a mechanical drive to one axle only. The balancing wheels running along the bottom of the rail steered the associated carrying wheel. The unit was usually driverless, with the control levers easy to reach by a waiting workman, or trips could be bolted in holes in the rails to automatically stop the unit. With rails supported at the ends by adjustable stands only every ten feet (on straights) its ease of laying track over rough ground is obvious.

The next application I saw was in April 1964 during the construction of a new bridge near the oil depot in St James, Northampton, by W.French. Their units were later models, with hydraulic drive to both bogies (note the oil pipe along the frame). Note also the ease of laying track on scaffolding.

The track system included points, with a foot pedal to lift the end of the switch rail before moving it by hand from one position to the other.

Drainage work near Wellingborough

During May 1964 the Conduit Construction Co. of Salford had a contract to construct four miles of drainage tunnel in Wellingborough in the meadows beside the River Ise. On 8th May Motor Rail 4813 of 1937 was at work (*below*) and nearby was Motor Rail 21287 of 1959 (*right*). By 10th July, the earlier Simplex, some wagons and a pile of prefabricated track was dumped beside Finedon Road (*bottom*).

Fellmongering in Northampton

Railways could be discovered unexpectedly, not least the hand-operated 2 ft gauge system used by the Co-operative Wholesale Society Fellmongering site, Rush Mills, Northampton, situated on an island in the River Nene near Beckett's Park. (SP758600). On 6th April, 1966 it was around 50 years old and had about 50 yards of track in the open, linking a store, seen in the photograph below, with what I noted as 'Works'. The open section included a narrow wooden bridge about 60 ft long over a river channel, with a wooden walkway between the rails for a man pushing the wagons (*below*). There were six wagons, basically flat trolleys to carry sheep skins with a chest high handrail at each end. The 'works' contained two small turntables to give access to a long siding. Wagon outside the 'works', with piles of sheep skins (*right*).

Fisons Basic Slag Ltd, Corby

Whether steel was to be made in a Bessemer or open hearth converter, lime was placed in the converter before pouring in liquid iron. The lime formed slag, removing many impurities from the steel, not least phosphorus, which made 'basic slag' valuable as a fertilizer. Corby then had a major steelworks, using locally quarried iron ore, and Fisons Basic Slag Ltd used the Bessemer slag bank for raw material. (SP902898). Periodically one of the standard gauge steelworks locomotives would take slag ladles, each holding at least 10 tons, to the top of the slag bank. There the wagons would be uncoupled from each other and the locomotive, and the end of the tipping chain placed on the neighbouring vehicle's drawhook. The tipping chain was anchored to the floor at one end of the slag ladle, and led round a floor pulley to a pulley just below the ladle's lip, back to another floor pulley to pass through a hole in the buffer beam and terminate in a large ring, with sufficient slack to permit attachment to the next wagon. When all was ready the locomotive slowly reversed, tightening the chain on the first ladle which pulled the ladle vertical. The liquid slag poured out and flowed down the bank, like emptying a large bucket of red hot water. As the locomotive continued to move the chains tightened and the second ladle tipped. It had had longer to cool so it turned out as a solid, but burst on hitting the ground, sending molten slag flying. The last ladle had longest to cool and turned out as a pyramidal lump which bounced down the side of the slag bank. Very spectacular to watch!

0-6-0ST No. 22 Robert Stephenson & Hawthorns 6944 of 1940 with 4 ladles, but the one nearest the locomotive seems to have been a spacer, for the heat, note the tipping chains.

Fisons' 2 ft gauge railway was a single track along the bottom of the slag bank. All taken 13th June, 1964. (*See also inside back cover*).

A small face shovel dug the slag and loaded it into trains of seven V-skips. Only six skips were loaded, the one next to the locomotive being left empty as a spacer to prevent the excavator bucket accidentally hitting the locomotive.

One locomotive, formerly two, was in daily use and the others were in the shed close to the tip where the slag went to be ground for fertilizer. The shed was unusual in that it had no rail access, but was within the area served by an overhead crane, so locomotives must have been lifted 'on and off shed'. In the photograph below, there are two spare locomotives, a train being tipped, and part of the overhead crane's gantry is visible.

Parkinson Industrial Buildings Ltd, Wellingborough

Following the closure of Wellingborough Ironworks in October 1962, part of the site (close to the former calcining bank) was used by Parkinson Industrial Buildings Ltd for a works to manufacture prefabricated panels for buildings (SP899694) visited 1st September, 1965 before the plant was fully operational. A 3 ft gauge railway was laid round three sides of the works building, through a loop, and extended into a stock yard. Three cranes spanned different places on the line. The railway was operated by two relatively new cabless Ruston Hornsby diesels, 3531 & 3532, respectively 466588 & 466589, both of 1961, 31hp class LBT, transferred from another Sir Lindsay Parkinson site.

Both sides of the Ruston Hornsby diesel locomotives seen in the loop.

On my visit in September 1965, there were ten 3 ft gauge bolster wagons.

A 2 ft gauge hand-operated line ran right round the works, having turntables at the corners, with four flat wagons.

Also in the works was a 5 ft gauge section, with ten unusual flat wagons with their width considerably more than their length.

Gannister mining, Cranford

Tonks' book caused me to go via the ironstone quarries at Cranford on my way to the Broads. Not only were there some well kept standard gauge locomotives but also a disused 2 ft gauge one, formerly used to work beds of ganister (silica sand used for furnace lining) overlying the ironstone. I found *Pixie*, a Bagnall 0-4-0ST, 2090 of 1919, in poor condition abandoned in its shed. (SP929778) Who would have thought then that it would be purchased by Rev E.R. 'Teddy' Boston, restored and I would see it in use on his railway in the rectory garden only five years later!

Above: *Pixie* abandoned at Cranford, 24th March, 1960.

Left: Footplate of *Pixie*, in the shed.

Below: Restored and running in the rectory garden at Cadeby, Leicestershire, 19th June, 1965.

Ironstone quarries, Desborough

Desborough Co-operative Society opened an ironstone quarry using standard gauge equipment in 1905, and its two locomotives survived at Irchester Quarries until the 1960s, although the Co-op quarry was closed in the 1920s. However, British Gas Purifying Materials Co. Ltd began operations, extracting ironstone from near the former Co-op ones (SP797829). The ironstone was taken by 2 ft gauge railway to a plant where it was ground and heated, and then bagged for dispatch to gas works in standard gauge wagons. (In old gas works coal was heated in the absence of air to drive off gases. Unfortunately these gases contained a lot of sulphur, but passing them through trays of iron ore removed the sulphur, enabling the clean gas to be piped to consumers. The sulphur rich iron ore was then used elsewhere to manufacture sulphuric acid.) The railway had two Hunslet 4wD, 1975 of 1939 (green) and 2459 of 1941 (orange), which hauled trains of six or seven V-skips. Their cabs were removed during fine weather. Until 1964, when an excavator was introduced, the ore was loaded by hand, but weekly output was only about 50 tons. In the upper photograph, Hunslet 1975 and train, 30th October, 1961. The lower one shows the elevated tipping dock on a gantry at the works, with its low roof, and planks beside the rails for the men tipping the wagons.

Isebrook Quarry, Burton Latimer

Thomas E.Gray & Co. Ltd at Isebrook Quarry, Burton Latimer, had a 2 ft gauge line operated by two Motor Rail diesels, 9411 of 1948 (in photograph taken 18th May 1965) and 5881 of 1935, which hauled V-skips of ganister sand from the quarry to a tip where the sand was tipped into internal use only standard gauge wagons which a Sentinel steam locomotive took to the works for processing. (SP892755)

Ironworks, Hunsbury Hill, Northampton

Until 1921 there had been an ironworks beside the railway to Blisworth, obtaining ore from nearby Hunsbury Hill, on the southern edge of Northampton. When I lived in that town expansion was under discussion but Hunsbury Hill was then farmland westwards from about quarter mile east of the line of the main line railway's tunnel. As a result, remains of the 3 ft 8 in. gauge quarry railway were still visible, a cutting and embankment near Rothersthorpe Road, a clear line across fields and a bridge under what was then A43 Towcester Road. The photograph (27th April, 1963) shows the route across the top of Hunsbury Hill, with Dane's Camp in the background. Track was later laid here by the Northamptonshire Ironstone Railway Trust.

The bridge under Towcester Road at SP742578. Note the field below road level, typical in quarrying areas, and the rock face of the last workings at this place, 15th April, 1965.

Years later, when the Northamptonshire Ironstone Railway Trust was clearing their site, a length of 3 ft 8 in. gauge track was discovered. Taken 1st August, 1976, with the author's mother, wife and son.

Ironstone Mine, Irthlingborough

Richard Thomas & Baldwins Ltd operated an ironstone mine about half a mile south-west of Irthlingborough (SP940697). A double track 3 ft gauge railway ran along the adit, with overhead electric locomotives for haulage out to the yard. In the early 1960s the local Inspector of Mines required changes in the overhead system, and it was cheaper to convert the overhead locomotives to battery operation. Once in the yard the train was left in one of several reception sidings and the locomotive was uncoupled and moved to the empty wagon area. The loaded wagons were moved first by continuous cable between the rails and then by a creeper (an endless chain between the rails which engaged the wagon axles) until they could be run individually over a weighbridge and into a rotary tippler. After emptying the wagon ran down a steeply graded track, over a trailing point to a steeply graded uphill track, which caused the wagon to reverse direction and run into the empties track.

The first two overhead locomotives were built by General Electric in the USA in 1916 but unlike the later Greenwood & Batley locomotives they were not rebuilt for battery operation. The rebuilt locomotives carried a small battery which enabled them to run round the train and do shunting, while batteries carried in the bogie 'tender' provided enough power for a day's use hauling trains. Within the pillar and stall workings of the mine small battery locomotives were always used. The first ones were built by British Electric Vehicles.

Overhead electric locomotive No. 6 Greenwood & Batley 1746 of 1941, leaves the mine adit, 21st August, 1958. (*see also inside back cover*).

Weighbridge in foreground, pair of rotary tipplers, empties track visible on left through fence, 22nd November, 1965.

South end of the yard, 22nd November, 1965, with tracks for loaded wagons on right with tipplers in the distance, and empties tracks on the left. Note continuous cable haulage on each track. On each side of each empties track was a rotating device with four nozzles to automatically grease wagon wheels as they came past. In the far distance is the spire of Rushden church.

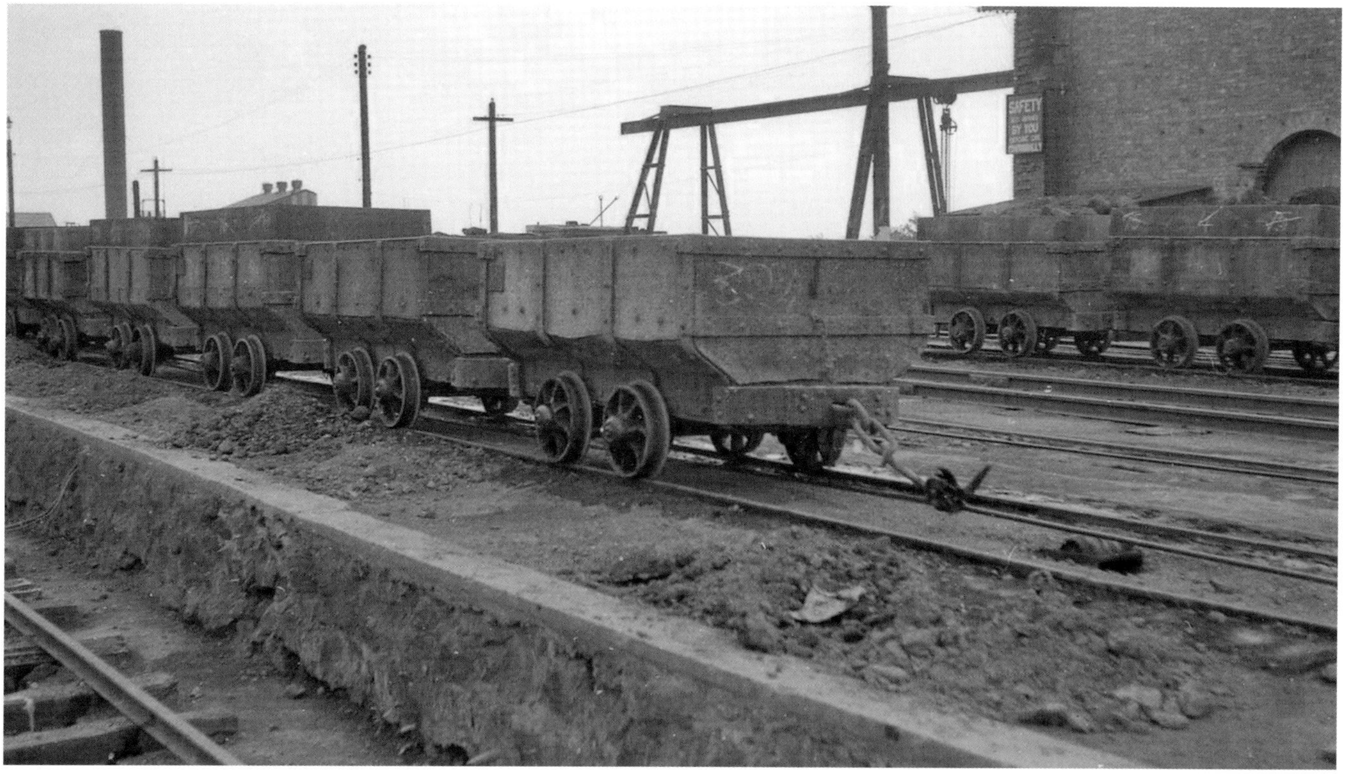

A train of empty wagons under cable haulage, 27th June, 1965. Note the haulage clip attaching the wagon to the cable, with its handle to fasten or release it; and the tubs with raised sides to facilitate machine loading.

No. 2 GEC (USA) 6099 of 1916 and No. 5 GB 1567 of 1937 behind, probably obscuring the other GEC locomotive. Note the neatly stacked hand-loaded ore in the wagons and the haulage cable. 21st August, 1958.

No. 4 GB 1566 of 1938 in the yard, 21st May, 1964.

No. 5 GB 1567 of 1938, as rebuilt for battery operation in March 1962, 21st May, 1964, with its battery tender and small on-board battery.

No. 3 BEV 156 of 1919, seen in the yard on 21st August, 1958. The ore tubs nominally held 3 tons, but careful stacking when loading by hand permitted 3½ tons to be carried. Once mechanical loaders were introduced in the late 1940s the tubs were progressively fitted with side extensions so the same load could be carried, as on the tubs in the background. Over time larger mines locomotives were introduced.

No. 95 GB 2295 of 1950. Note the bell on the locomotive, the wagons for explosives, and the derailment in the distance. 21st August, 1958.

No. 5 running round its battery tender, while Ruston Hornsby 478764, with exhaust conditioner for use underground, stands on the left. Behind is the new battery charging shed, 21st May 1964.

Inside the battery charging shed, 21st May, 1965. A number of additional Ruston Hornsby mines diesel locomotives (some 2 ft 6 in. gauge for spares) were transferred to Irthlingborough from mines in Cleveland, North Yorkshire, in 1962, in case of problems arising during the change to main line battery operation. Here are a lot of them stored in the battery charging shed.

One of the newcomers, RH 418803 of 1957, standing in the yard. Note the exhaust conditioner behind the cab to reduce fumes underground, 22nd November, 1965.

Man rider, made by permanently coupling two mine tubs, taking out the ends and fitting seats. 22nd November, 1965

Abandoned in a siding was an unusual steel bodied side tipping wagon with a wood frame, said to have been used when the site was being developed 22nd November, 1965.

Kettering Iron & Coal Co. Ltd

On the west side of the Midland main line, about a mile north of Kettering station, was the ironworks of the Kettering Iron & Coal Co. Ltd (SP860800), using ore from the company's quarries some two miles further west towards Rothwell, carried by a delightful 3 ft gauge railway. When the ironworks closed in April 1959 the quarries remained in operation until October 1962, sending ore by British Railways to nearby Corby.

The narrow gauge system had three Manning Wardle 0-6-0ST used for main line haulage and two Black Hawthorn 0-4-0ST for shunting at the works, although they did occasionally go to the quarries.

The yard, with *Kettering Furnaces No. 7* (foreground) and *Kettering Furnaces No. 2* behind. The ironworks is still standing although out of use. The hoists took tall barrows of ore etc for loading into the top of the furnaces, 5th July, 1960.

There was also an unusual Sentinel steam locomotive, with a vertical boiler in each cab and a vertical steam engine under the outer end of each bonnet, with a chain drive to the axles, which was out of use when I saw it on 11th January, 1960. Usually two 0-6-0ST and one 0-4-0ST were in use daily.

When I first visited the railway ore was still excavated by hand, but I did not record that as I should have done! The only photograph I have is the one above taken on 11th January, 1960, showing *Kettering Furnaces No. 8* (Manning Wardle 1675 of 1906) in the quarry. Note the sledge hammer and crowbar to loosen the ore just behind the locomotive, and the multi-prong fork, on the right, level with the buffer beam, to load it. Note also the long line of wagons along the quarry. I assume groups of two or three were left at intervals along the face for each gang of men, and then when the locomotives returned the first would remove half of the filled wagons, the other would remove the remainder and distribute the empties before returning to the works.

Latterly the two main line locomotives in use made three return trips, two in the morning and one in the afternoon. The first one went under the main Rothwell road and left its train, with the rear wagon spragged, in a loop at the entrance to the quarry. The photograph above shows empties brought by No. 8 in the quarry loop. Note the sprag (brake stick) thrust through the spokes of the last wagon. 8th January, 1962. The locomotive then went into the quarry to collect loaded wagons.

Kettering Furnaces No. 6, MW 1123 of 1889, at quarry entrance on 8th January, 1962.

By 8th January, 1962, an excavator had been brought to dig the ore, (*see also the back cover*) but there was still plenty of manual effort required. Once a wagon had been filled it had to be moved out of the way, by man power, for the next empty. Sometimes the excavator driver positioned his bucket behind the wagon and then gradually slewed his machine, starting the wagon moving. This practice no doubt accounted for many of the broken wagon body end planks in the later days! Like those on wagon No. 134.

Eventually the rake of empty wagons was some distance away, so the excavator was used to bring them nearer. The driver slewed his machine and racked out its dipper arm towards the wagons. A length of wire rope was then hooked to the leading wagon and the back of the excavator bucket. Slewing the excavator then drew the rake of wagons nearer the loading position. Unfortunately the 6 ft length of wire rope does not show up very well in the photograph, 8th January, 1962. When the locomotive returned it was coupled to the loaded wagons and drew them forward until it had a train of 24 wagons.

Kettering Furnaces No. 8 waiting while the last wagons are filled. The dragline in the distance removed overburden, dumping it in worked out areas. 30th April, 1962.

The locomotive then took its train under the main road and waited in the loop just beyond the bridge for the second train of empties to arrive. *Kettering Furnaces No. 6* in the loop waiting for *Kettering Furnaces No. 7* to arrive, 8th January, 1962. The first locomotive then departed with its train for the works, leaving the second to collect the next rake of full wagons and take all the empties into the quarry.

The main line ran through the fields, with a cutting where it went under a lane. *Kettering Furnaces No. 7* MW 1370 of 1897 has just passed under the lane, 30th October, 1961.

One of my memories is the sight of a train of pale wagons on the skyline near the works. *Kettering Furnaces No. 6*, Manning Wardle 1123 of 1889, 8th January, 1962. It was not difficult to watch a train leave the quarry loop then chase it by bicycle to vantage points on its journey.

When a loaded train was expected, the works shunter went into a siding and waited for it to pass. *Kettering Furnaces No. 2* (Black Hawthorn 501 of 1879) waits in the siding for *Kettering Furnaces No. 8* and its train to pass, 11th January, 1960. Once the train had passed the shunter accelerated out of the siding and buffered up to the rear of the moving train. Meanwhile the train engine had uncoupled at some point and accelerated away to the far side of the tipping dock. Points were changed rapidly and the loaded train was pushed into the near side of the tip. This burst of activity could well be because the small locomotive could not start and then push a loaded train round the sharp 90° curve and on to the tip. Whatever the reason, it was good to watch!

When the ironworks had been in operation the ore had been calcined before use. The tip comprised a series of brick walls spanned by girders carrying three tracks and their walkways, thus forming a series of compartments. Each compartment had been filled in turn, assisted by the presence of three tracks, and layers of small coal were tipped on to layers of ore. When full a compartment was set on fire and left to burn for a long time. When the ore had been calcined, which changed it chemically and the colour turned from sandy brown to brick red, men dug it out and loaded barrows to charge the furnaces. At any time some compartments were being filled, some were on fire and some were being emptied. Following closure of the ironworks part of the calcine tip was demolished and a hole knocked through the remaining compartment walls so a standard gauge siding could be laid. Ore was then tipped direct into main line wagons for transport to Corby. Note demolition ball in foreground, 11th January, 1960.

Occasionally all three 0-6-0ST were in use, one acting as works shunter, as here 30th October 1961, with (left to right) *Kettering Furnaces No. 7* (shunting on tip, unusual), *Kettering Furnaces No. 8* and *Kettering Furnaces No. 6*.

Kettering Furnaces No. 3 BH 859 of 1885 on the tip, 8th January, 1962.

Kettering Furnaces No 3 shunting. Weather protection for the driver was minimal! Kettering is in the distance, and an internal wagon lettered KF is in the mid-ground on the right hand edge. The points for the branch to the lower engine shed are just beyond the locomotive. 8th January, 1962.

Kettering Furnaces No. 2 outside the upper shed, with a new boiler for one of the standard gauge fleet in the distance. 11th January, 1960.

Kettering Furnaces No. 7 near the water tank, 11th January, 1960.

The Sentinel, out of use, outside the lower shed which had both narrow and standard gauge tracks. The tank and cab of a standard gauge Andrew Barclay lie on the right in the background, 11th January, 1960.

Single-side tipping wagons for ore. Note the simple catch to secure the door – knocking it upwards as the wagons went on to the tip opened the door in readiness for tipping, 24th March, 1959.

As the ore is removed so the face recedes, and the track has to be moved forward, 8th January, 1962.

Replenishing locomotive coal, note K.I.&.C.Co. ownership plate on the cab. I expect coal for calcining was loaded into tipping wagons the same way, 8th January, 1962.

Quarrying ceased on 24th October, 1962 and the railway was dismantled. I managed to get time off work to visit for the last time. It was very sad seeing men I recognised destroying their railway. There was an intermediate loop on the main line, near the furthest tree in the top photo page 38, and here was the demolition team's hut, brought along on a pair of tipper underframes, Tuesday 20th November, 1962. Unfortunately I then discovered the locomotive was only used on Mondays, Wednesdays and Fridays so I had to get a second day off the following week to see it!

Lifting was at the loop nearby close to the main road. The track and sleepers were lifted a few inches by a jack so the spikes could be withdrawn by simply hitting the sleepers with a sledge hammer, Monday, 26th November.

A pickaxe was then put into one of the fishplate holes to lever the freed rail onto its side.

Chalk and a stick the right length were used to mark along the foot the places to cut the rail, and an oxyacetylene burner was then used to cut the foot and web, but not the head, at each mark. When every mark had been cut then a man went along the rail giving a sharp blow with a sledge at each cut, which caused the head there to fracture. The short lengths were then stacked in a wagon.

Kettering Furnaces No. 7 on the track lifting train, 26th November, 1962. The wagons have had new door planks fitted. The locomotive only worked Monday, Wednesday and Friday, so had to leave sufficient empty wagons nearby for the lifting gang to use on the other days. Shunting to manoeuvre the full and empty wagons was done in the nearby loop. The train then returned to the works.

Some sleepers were also loaded and subsequently dumped in a cutting by the bridge under a lane, 26th November, 1962.

Compare the lifted trackbed looking under Rothwell road towards the quarry, 20th November, 1962, with the top picture on page 38.

Kettering Furnaces No.3 went to the National Trust for preservation at Penrhyn Castle, Bangor, North Wales, while *Kettering Furnaces No. 8* was initially preserved, along with a tipping wagon from Scaldwell Quarries, by Kettering Borough Council in Manor House Gardens, photographed there on 11th April, 1964. In 1974 it went to the Welland Valley Traction Engine Club at Market Harborough where, in 2020, it is 'currently under restoration'.

Ironstone quaries, Hanging Houghton

The Lamport Quarries of Staveley Iron & Chemical Co. Ltd were about seven miles north of Northampton. The main line railway to Market Harborough ran northwards along the floor of a wide valley, with the main road some three quarters of a mile to the east and 150 feet above it, just beyond the top of the valley sides. Two quarry sites were opened here in 1913, Hanging Houghton Quarries close to the edge of the valley and Scaldwell Quarries about a mile further east. Both quarries had similar 3 ft gauge railways, which brought the ore to the same aerial ropeway which carried it down to the main line.

A similar ropeway carrying clay to a brickworks at Fletton, Peterborough, 25th March, 1960. Lattice steel towers at regular intervals support two heavy stationary cables on which the buckets with small grooved wheels run. A lighter continuous cable hauls the buckets. At each end of the ropeway, and anywhere it was necessary to change direction, were large steel structures with rails to carry the buckets, horizontal wheels to guide the haulage cable, and probably hanging heavy weights to tension the carrying cables.

Left: During the Second World War to facilitate increased production a steeply graded standard gauge line was laid up the valley side to serve Hanging Houghton Quarries visible on the left in the background. The narrow gauge locomotives were transferred to Scaldwell Quarries, and the rest just abandoned. The photograph shows the remains of the tipping dock where 3 ft gauge wagons were emptied into ropeway buckets. The later standard gauge line is in the left background. 19th April, 1960. SP751730.

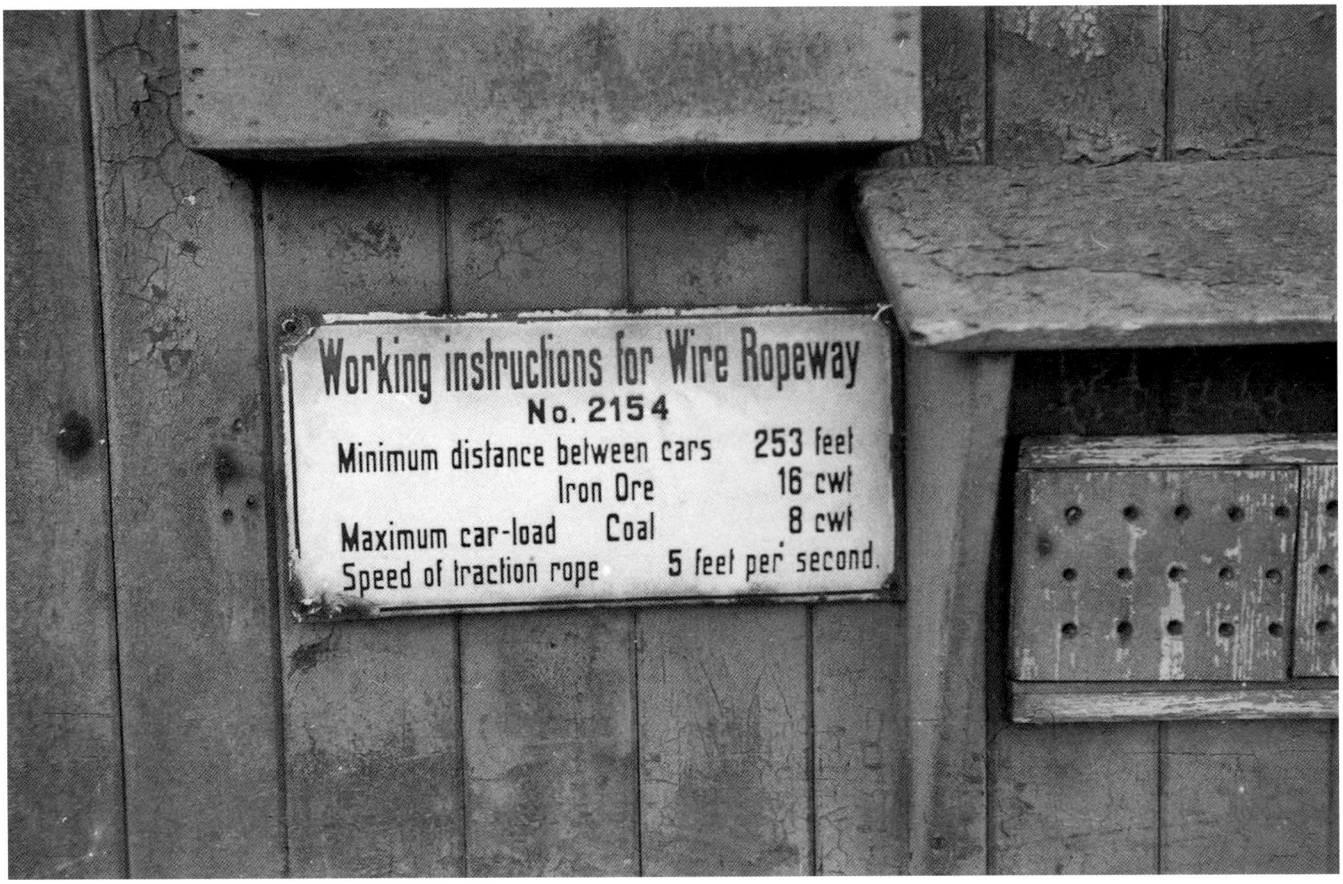

A plate giving instructions for ropeway staff was still attached to a wall, 19th April, 1960.

I first visited this place on 19th March, 1959. Side tipping ore wagons stood on the embankment to the tip, and a couple of unusual end tippers, possibly dating from construction of the embankment, were also present. The trees provided a wind break in an otherwise exposed spot.

A double hedge hid more side tippers, 19th March, 1960; winter and early spring were the best times to visit, when there were no leaves!

An unusual homemade wagon with wooden bogies, possibly to carry an excavator jib, 10th December, 1961.

Scaldwell Quarries

My first visit to Scaldwell Quarries was in August 1955, soon after I came to Northampton. The ropeway was then standing, although out of use, as a standard gauge extension had been laid from the Hanging Houghton line to a new tipping dock on the outskirts of Scaldwell. (SP766720) The upper photograph from 31st August, 1955, shows the ropeway terminus, which housed the steam haulage engine. On the extreme left is the cutting to give clearance to the buckets on the two carrying cables. In the foreground are rails to carry spare buckets (note their small grooved wheels) with, on the right, empty buckets waiting to pass under the filling chute, and the hinged flap of a point to transfer buckets to and from the siding. On the far right is the wooden hopper for ore, and the chute to load the buckets, with the 3 ft gauge on a wooden trestle. Behind is the shed where the locomotive *Handyman* rested. The lower picture, taken during the IRS farewell visit on 17th August, 1963 (the railway and quarries having closed in December 1962), shows the steel supports for the former ropeway tipping dock, the cutting for the buckets, *Handyman* outside its shed and the offices in the distance.

The last quarries were towards Holcot, above Pitsford Reservoir. *Above*: A dragline stripped overburden and a face shovel loaded the wagons behind *Scaldwell* Peckett 1316 of 1913 (*see also front cover*), the railway being laid on the ore bed.

With one locomotive in steam daily, the normal train was nine wagons. Both 7th September, 1961.

The train overshot the new tip and reversed into the loop, where the wagons were spragged and the locomotive was uncoupled, 7th September, 1961. Meanwhile the rake of empties was released and ran by gravity onto the main line, coming to rest in the nearby dip, where the locomotive coupled on for the next trip to the quarry.

At the tip wagons were run in rakes of three to the tipping point, where they were stopped by spragging (the jammed wheel vibrated violently as the other wheel on the axle tried to rotate) and the wagon being tipped was clamped to the rails, 7th September, 1961. Note the spare sprags in the foreground.

A rake of three narrow gauge wagons filled one standard gauge side tipping dump car. The locomotive brought six dump cars at a time, left three in a loop to be run to the tip later by gravity, and waited while three were filled, then took them and the previously left rake of three down the hill to be tipped on the calcine clamp. 0-6-0ST *Lamport* No. 2 Bagnall 2669 of 1942, waiting while its dump cars are filled, with the 3 ft gauge above, 5th January, 1962. Some 200,000 tons of calcined ore had to be removed after the quarries closed.

General view of the tip, with the day's last rake of empty 3 ft wagons and a rake of dump cars ready for the first load of the next day, with the loop for waiting empties behind. 7th September, 1961.

Scaldwell yard with 3-way point leading to the shed and spare wagon sidings, 6th September, 1962.

Originally working at Hanging Houghton Quarries, and transferred to Scaldwell after their closure, *Lamport*, Peckett 1315 of 1913, stands outside the shed and coal stage at Scaldwell, with the offices behind. The long water tank with curved ends was typical in the ironstone quarries, 4th July, 1960.

Handyman Hudswell Clarke 573 of 1900, in the sunlight, having been taken from its shed for the IRS visit on 17th August, 1963.

Spare wagons. Note the angle-iron strengthening the corner at the opening side, the catches to hold the body closed (levered off with a crowbar) and the sprag in the wheel. 17th August, 1963.

Opening side of a wagon. Again note angle-iron strengthening. 17th August, 1963.

One Friday evening, 20th March, 1964, after a day when I had travelled to the client by train, I was cycling home from the station along St Peter's Way (effectively the inner ring road) when I saw the unmistakable outline of a saddle tank locomotive ahead of me. Weaving through the rush hour traffic I soon caught it up, and found *Scaldwell* en route to Brockham, near Dorking, Surrey, for preservation. And I had no camera with me! But the traffic was slow, I was on a bike, and I knew that Scaldwell would have to pass the end of my road, so I pedalled home like mad, tore into the house, shouted a greeting to my wife of six months and "Back in a minute!", grabbed my camera, and hurtled back to the end of the road. I was just in time! and caught it for this photograph, in London Road Northampton.

Wellingborough Ironworks

Wellingborough Ironworks stood in the north-west angle where Finedon Road (A510) crossed the Midland Railway main line from St Pancras to Derby, obtaining its ore from quarries on Finedon hill. Although the ironworks closed in October 1962 the quarries with their metre gauge railway continued in operation until October 1966. The ironworks and railway had been modernized in the early 1930s, giving a system equipped like no other ironstone line. Latterly it was operated by Stewarts & Lloyds Minerals Ltd.

The railway left the ironworks by a tunnel under the main line and reached the brick built shed. In the upper photograph, Peckett 1871 of 1934 is entering the shed yard (SP 905695) with a train of empties, the rear still being in the tunnel, 7th July, 1960. After a level section across the floor of the River Ise valley there was a long climb – about three quarters of a mile – up to the quarries, crossing Finedon Road on the way. In the lower picture Peckett 2029 of 1942 approaches Findon Road crossing, 24th March, 1960. All of the 0-6-0ST, at that time, were un-numbered.

The gradient eased for the actual crossing, with Peckett 2029, 24th March, 1960. (*see also back cover*)

Latterly, the locomotive working in the quarries went down to the shed at lunchtime, and afterwards the first train of empties had double power, with No. 85 Peckett 1870, with No. 86 Peckett 1871 banking, 3rd November, 1965. One of the two locomotives in steam daily worked the main line, from works to sidings at the top of the hill, while the other took two or three wagons at a time into the deep quarries, which were well supervised and I never entered them.

For the downhill run back to the works the photograph shows the brakes on the leading wagons were pinned down, and released (I assume) near the river bridge.

At the bottom of the hill was a bridge over the River Ise. Peckett 2029 is crossing, with all wagon brakes now off, both 7th July, 1960.

No. 86, Peckett 1871, crossing the River Ise, 3rd November, 1965.

No. 87 Peckett 2029 leaving the tunnel under the Midland main line. Note check rail and bullhead rail in chairs on this section. 1st September, 1965.

When the railway was modernized one of the former locomotives survived as works shunter, *Wellingborough No. 4*, Hunslet 473 of 1888, but was withdrawn and scrapped in October 1959, it is seen here dumped, and overgrown, behind the shed, 29th October, 1956.

Pecketts 1871 of 1934 – later No. 86 – and 2029 of 1942 – later No. 87 – outside the shed, 7th July, 1960. The wagons on the right are in the BR yard.

The section from the tunnel to the unloading area was uphill. It was laid with concrete sleepers and provided with a catch point in case of runaways, 1st September, 1965.

In the unloading area a crane with a special sling lifted the skips of ore and emptied them by inversion. Originally this had been done in the ironworks but later the ore was emptied into standard gauge wagons for transport to Corby. In the distance a skip has just been lifted off its wagon, one of a full rake headed by No. 87, 1st September, 1965. (*see also inside front cover*).

Ore being emptied into standard gauge wagon. I think the steps in the background were to enable the allegedly empty BR wagons to be checked before filling, in case a significant amount of ore had remained stuck in one, 1st September, 1965.

No. 85 Peckett 1870 of 1934, with spark arrester on chimney outside the shed, 5th May, 1965.

No. 86, Peckett 1871 also with spark arrester, 5th May, 1965.

No. 86 near coaling stage, 6th May, 1965.

Coaling No. 87 Peckett 2029 with shed and BR wagons behind, 26th November, 1964.

Peckett 2029 – no running number yet – in shed yard, tunnel and ironworks behind, 15th July, 1957.

Peckett 2029, now No. 87, 5th May, 1965. All three Pecketts are now preserved by Irchester Narrow Gauge Trust at Irchester Country Park.

Ore wagons. Note brake levers, axleboxes, central buffer coupling and 'teeth' on circular lifting frame to grip the unloading sling. 10th July, 1964.

Ore wagon frame used as basis of permanent way flat wagon for sleepers, 5th May, 1965

Wagon for locomotive ash on ore wagon frame. The central buffer coupler is clearly visible, 26th November, 1964.

Bassett-Lowke Ltd, Northampton

The head office, shop and works of Bassett-Lowke Ltd, model makers, was at 18-25 Kingswell Street, Northampton (SP753603), a narrow street off Gold Street and parallel to Bridge Street. A catalogue dated around 1960 listed gauge 'O' (1/43 scale) railway equipment and components, as well as components for ship modellers and model engineers. It even offered castings and drawings for a 'Royal Scot' 4-6-0 in 7¼ in. gauge (1/8 scale) with the note 'We will be pleased to quote for the finished model'. While this might have been optimistic in 1960, from 1904 until the Second World War Bassett-Lowke had constructed large models for passenger haulage on 7¼ in. (1/8 scale), 9½ or 10 ¼ in. (1/6 scale) and 15 in. (1/4 scale) gauge railways in gardens, parks and exhibitions. A relic of those days formed part of the shop window display in October 1964. A model house and garden (in 1/48 scale) had a railway in its garden, with a typical 4-4-2 hauling wagons which could have carried people 'showing the possibilities of 7¼ and 9½ gauges and equipment'.

Eastwell & Loddington Ironstone Co. Ltd

Three miles west of Kettering is Loddington which had quarries west of the village, once served by a metre gauge system owned by Eastwell & Loddington Ironstone Co. Ltd. This was closed in August 1958, before I knew the site existed, and it was replaced by a standard gauge system. My photographs were all taken after closure, but I have obtained some shots of the line when in use.

Latterly there were two locomotives. One was *J.D.Ellis* 0-4-0ST Sharp Stewart 2298 of 1873, seen with a train of the distinctive wagons. It was scrapped in early 1959.   *Harry Townley, IRS collection via Kevin Lane*

By the time I made my first visit little remained of it, just a coupling rod and some small bits dumped in a wagon, 11th January, 1960. Quite a few wagons still stood in the yard. The line to the tip, situated just beyond the hut, ran on the embankment behind them.

The second, much larger, locomotive *William Ellis* 0-6-0ST Avonside 2054 of 1930, slumbered in its shed until cut up in 1966.

William Ellis in use.   *Frank Jones, Andrew Neale collection*

Loddington also saw the use of French-built *Cambrai*, Corpet Louvet & Cie 493 of 1888, which had been purchased from the C de F du Cambresis in 1936. It was transferred to the company's Waltham Quarries near Belvoir Castle, Leicestershire, in March 1956. *Cambrai* is now preserved by the Irchester Narrow Gauge Railway Trust in Irchester Country Park, a former ironstone quarry.
Kevin Lane collection

General view of the yard looking towards the quarries, with a rake of loaded wagons waiting on a slight down gradient to go on the tippler, the empties running back by gravity on the other track.
Harry Townley, IRS collection via Kevin Lane

The wagons were steel tubs, holding about 1½ tons of ore, emptied by inversion in a rotary tippler. This photograph (*above*) shows the remains of the Loddington tippler which emptied into BR wagons brought along a branch line from Kettering, 11th January, 1960.

The metre gauge system at Waltham Quarries, Leicestershire, had similar tubs and the photographs (*centre and left*) show the tippler after that line's closure, 20th April 1960. The axis of rotation was at ground level, and there was a heavy weight underneath to bring the tippler upright with an empty tub, but not so heavy as to prevent the tippler overbalancing with a loaded tub once the brake was released.

Islip quarries

Although strictly outside my time frame, as the system closed in 1952 four years before I lived in the area, it is worth mentioning the largest 3 ft gauge ironstone railway, which served the Islip Quarries, SP 969782, of Stewarts & Lloyds Minerals Ltd near Thrapston. Several members of its unusual and once extensive fleet of about ten locomotives are illustrated. Those supplied new (5, 6, & 8 are shown) were cut down due to limited clearances in places.

No. 4 Bagnall 1563 of 1899, April 1950.   *Frank Jones, Andrew Neale collection*

No. 5 0-4-0T Bagnall 1946 of 1911, July, 1949.   *Ken Cooper, via K.Lane, IRS collection*

No.6 Dick Kerr of 1918, April 1950. *Frank Jones, Andrew Neale collection*

No. 8 Kilmarnock Engineering 510 of 1920, April 1950. *Frank Jones, Andrew Neale collection*

No. 0-4-2ST No. 9 Hudswell Clarke 1087 of 1914 in July 1949. This locomotive had been purchased originally by the Earls Barton Iron Ore Co. Ltd, whose site was later worked by Earls Barton Silica Co. Ltd (*see page 80*).
Ken Cooper, via K.Lane, IRS collection

No. 11 *Dike* Hudswell Clarke 1452 of 1921, with a part of one of the unusual hopper wagons used.
Frank Jones, April 1950. Andrew Neale collection

Billing Aquadrome

Billing Aquadrome, situated about three miles east of Northampton, was and is a holiday park close to the River Nene (SP808615). It was constructed around worked out gravel pits. A 10¼ in. gauge line here, with a red Royal Scot 4-6-0 operated here for several years after 1949. This was later replaced by a 2 ft gauge line, initially using equipment reclaimed from local gravel pits, like the Simplex with home-made body and roof with a train of articulated coaches, apparently using V-skip underframes for bogies in the upper photograph from 10th May, 1962. By 19th May, 1965 a Ruston Hornsby diesel, 242887 of 1946, was the motive power (*lower*). The train used to be stored close to the entrance, so it was easy enough at quiet times to walk in and photograph it, but I never explored the railway. I think it made a loop around a lake. The railway still exists, and has had a variety of motive power since I knew it.

Wicksteed Park, Kettering

The pleasure railway at Wicksteed Park, on the south-eastern outskirts of Kettering, (SP883770) probably dates from 1931 when Baguley supplied two steam outline 0-4-0PM locomotives, *Lady of the Lake* and *King Arthur* (2042 & 2043 of 1931, respectively). They were later fitted with Perkins diesel engines. The 'boiler' contains cooling water instead of having a radiator.

King Arthur, is seen on the right, with the mechanical transmission from the engine near the cab to the front jackshaft clearly visible, also the 4-ring Perkins logo, 6th July, 1962. Lakeside Railway train hauled by *King Arthur* at the station (*below*).

Later, Motor Rail supplied a standard 40S diesel locomotive, 22224 of 1966 *Cheyenne*, disguised with an American outline, photographed at the station on 16th August, 1968. It was this firm's only formal product for the leisure market, although many other disguised Simplex locomotives exist elsewhere. The route ran around a lake.

Sand & Aggregate extraction, Earls Barton

Earls Barton is a large village about half way between Northampton and Wellingborough. On the eastern edge of the village the Earls Barton Silica Co. Ltd worked the white silica sand which overlay the bed of iron ore once worked by the Earls Barton Iron Ore Co. Ltd (*see page 77*). (SP857640) The short railway took sand from the quarry either direct to a lorry tip or to a mill where it was crushed.

In the upper photograph Orenstein & Koppel 7595 of 1937 brings a train out of the quarry, 27th April, 1962. Later a Motor Rail Simplex, was obtained (*see title page*). As on most quarry railways, empties were pushed to the quarry and full wagons hauled back, but there was no loop at Earls Barton and wagons had to be pushed up a steep gradient to the mill so a wire rope was used to enable the locomotive to run round its train. In the lower photograph the driver of MR 8731 of 1941 has fastened a wire rope from the front of his locomotive to the rear of the first skip. Once the locomotive is on the siding the points can be changed and the wagons hauled onto the other track. The building behind served as an engine shed, 14th July, 1965.

OK 7595 taking two wagons up to the mill. The lorry tip was at the end of the lower line. The shunting rope lies on the ground, 27th April, 1962.

A common feature of industrial railways was the practice of leaving withdrawn locomotives dumped somewhere, and often left for years. Earls Barton Silica had such a dump. Photographed on 27th April, 1962, Lister petrol 10063 of 1938 lies in the weeds on a siding beyond the engine shed.

Beside the Lister was *Big Tom*, Ruston Hornsby 163997 of 1931. At the time I did not know, but this was the prototype of the common and successful small Ruston Hornsby diesel locomotives, and really should have been preserved instead of going for scrap in 1964.

Lying nearby was a Ruston cab, presumably off *Big Tom*, still bearing the Ruston Hornsby crest. Somewhere it had obviously worked somewhere where there was a limited clearance, shown by the unusual shape of the cab body.

The wagons were a mainly Allen (of Tipton) 'Eezitip' with a few by Robert Hudson, Leeds. These were unusual, being fitted with trunnions to permit a crane to lift a loaded body, and feet so the body could be put down on the ground and yet remain upright. Orenstein & Koppel 7595 and a Hudson wagon with trunnions and feet, 14th July, 1964.

MR 8731 near the lorry tip, served by the line reached by turntables at the end of the sidings 16th June, 1964.

A mile south of the village was the premises of Earls Barton Sand & Gravel Co. Ltd (SP863621), later a subsidiary of Mixconcrete Aggregates Ltd. The railway was basic, a long single track from pit to works, where there was a siding, with a loop halfway, used for passing trains or for storing the second train if it was not in use.

No. 6 RH 260724 of 1948, with home-made cab at the tip, with its simple shelter, 15th July, 1964.

In 28th May, 1966 RH 260724 was dumped in the loop with spare wagons. The Northampton to Wellingborough railway is on the embankment behind.

RH 292887 of 1946, derailed, and 331264 of 1952 by the fuel tank, 15th July, 1964.

Aggregate extraction, Little Billing

Studying the OS map (sheet 133) for my new area I was intrigued by the many 'sidings or tramways' marked, not least around Corby. The nearest, which obviously had nothing to do with British Railways, was near Little Billing, about three miles from home. The map marked a railway roughly shaped like a '6' around a lake. (SP797612) I went to investigate. At the end of an unmade road was a long brick building with a flat roof. This housed the office, and I suspect mess room, stores etc, and there was probably a weighbridge outside. At the far end a ramp led up to the roof from ground level, with a 2 ft gauge track laid up it. Obviously the trains went up here to tip into lorries – there was no other gantry of any sort. Following the track I came to points, and eventually came to a train parked by the lake. Nearby was a dragline. Walking further, I reached the points and I was back to where I started. *Below*: Simplex 1 (I recorded no details) and train near the flooded quarry, with dragline probably mounted on a barge behind. 24th August, 1955. Looking at the modern OS map (sheet 152) this area is now either built on or part of Billing Aquadrome.

Aggregate extraction, Hardingstone Junction Northampton

Ransome Road ran from London Road east, past the stables for Northampton Co-op Dairy Department (you should have heard a milk float with iron rims on its wheels, loaded with metal crates full of empty glass bottles, going flat out on a Sunday morning, with the roads empty of traffic and the horse knowing it was going home!) and the BR permanent way depot to finish at A.J.Mackaness Ltd's (later Mixconcrete Aggregates) Ransome Road Pits. (SP764593) Nearby, a footpath ran from beside the power station, over the railway at Hardingstone Junction, junction of the branches to Bedford and Wellingborough, to go south up the hill to Hardingstone. The railway was basically 'U' in plan, with the sides parallel to the main line railway along either side of the pit, with the depot at the end. When I knew it only the northern arm was in use. Sand and gravel were excavated by a RB-22 dragline with ¾ cubic yard bucket, emptying into a steel hopper spanning the track, so it could continue to dig while the train was away. Also, the hopper permitted a larger bucket than could conveniently be used to load skips directly. In the photograph below, 27th April, 1962, the excavator driver operates the hopper to fill wagons hauled by Simplex 8810 of 1943. The Bedford branch is on the embankment.

Quarry track is rarely well laid, and wagon derailments common so the locomotives often carried rerailing ramps. A derailed locomotive weighing 2½ tons presented more of a problem, as photographed here near the wagon storage loop, 27th April, 1962. Help was at hand! The chimneys and cooling tower of Northampton Power Station are in the background

The tip at the depot had quite a substantial shelter (winter winds whistled up the Nene valley, 'straight from the Ural Mountains' according to the locals!) and the hopper feeding the screening plant conveyor was covered with a coarse steel grid, to remove any large lumps, to break the fall of the load, and for operator safety. The corrugated-iron engine shed can be seen behind the pylon (it contained a second similar Simplex), with a wagon underframe carrying oil fuel for the excavator. 27th April, 1962.

Aggregate extraction, Little Houghton

Mackaness opened a new pit at Clifford Hill, near Little Houghton, some three miles east south-east of Northampton, on 24th September, 1962 (SP807602). There was an office and engine shed – which looked like a concrete garage – beside the lane from the village to Clifford Hill. The quarry railway turned sharply to run beside the Wellingborough branch, then swung out to dive under the branch to reach the pit, where again gravel was loaded into a hopper. Near the office was the tip, with a conveyor to load the gravel into hoppers, from which lorries took it to Ransome Road for screening. The track under the main line bridge was laid in concrete, but the rest was just laid on the ground. A single locomotive and seven V-skips were provided. A wire fence separated the office and shed area from the rest of the field, and a cattle grid was provided where the track ran through the fence. Construction was very simple, just a straight sided hole in the ground, 4 ft 6 in. long, 5 ft wide and 2 ft deep, spanned by unsupported rails.

MR 8810 and train crossing the cattle grid, Little Houghton signal box and crossing keeper's cottage behind. September 1962.

General view of Clifford Mill depot area, temporarily disused, with tip and shelter, conveyor for taking gravel up to the lorry loading hoppers, in the background office and just visible the empty engine shed. 4th April, 1966.

Aggregate extraction, St James End Northampton

F.E.Storton Ltd, St James End Gravel Pits, Weedon Road, Northamton (SP735604) were opened in early 1964. Like Mackaness' pits the other side of town it was taken over by Mixconcrete Aggregates in June 1965. The first line ran east from the tip some 270 yards to the pit. It was provided with a Simplex locomotive, 9204 of 1946 and eleven Hudson V-skips, numbered 1-14 (2, 3 & 8 missing), with six in use and the remainder stored nearby off the rails. A homemade wagon, comprising two 10 ft lengths of 3x7 in. steel channel, 35½ in. wide, and braced with angle-iron, with 3 ft wheelbase, was possibly used to carry track panels. *Upper:* Simplex 9204 and train stored at the tip after work, March 1964. Nearby is the wheeled frame, possibly used to carry track. The route to the pit crossed a stream by a bridge, 20 ft span and 7 ft wide, having a frame of 3x6 in. channel with two similar girders beneath the rails, and a floor of BR sleepers. A second Simplex came 23rd April, 1966. *Lower:* Motor Rail 9204 (*left*) and 8810 of 1943 (*right*) at the tip. Note boards to deflect falling gravel onto the conveyor and to prevent material falling in from the sides, 28th May, 1966.

For summer operation a line was laid westward in April or May 1968. It used the same tip, with one track pannel of the eastern line lifted to accommodate the new track which crossed the corner of the sunken conveyor hopper. After 200 yards was a loop with sprung points. MR 8739 of 1942 is at the loop, with another train ahead of it in the distance, 17th August, 1968.

Some 250 yards further was the pit, with the usual steel hopper for the excavator to fill. As the face receded, or when near areas had to be opened up, the hopper was dragged by the excavator, 17th August, 1968.

Excavator moving the steel hopper followed by two trains, 17th August, 1968.

From time to time, extra locomotives, sometimes just bought for spares, stood in the yard far from any rails. Like RH 371545 of 1954 photographed on 17th August, 1968 in the yard with a broken gearbox, with the tip behind. The eastern pits were worked out in 1969.

Sewage Works, Little Billing

The County Borough of Northampton had its sewage works at Little Billing (SP86618). Like many sewage works it once had an extensive 2 ft gauge railway to carry dried sludge to a tip in the nearby fields, but by May 1962 it shrunk to a very short line from the input screens which removed insoluble material to a tip. It was operated by a Lister petrol locomotive, 14006 of 1940 and a single end tipping wagon.

Above: Lister 14006 by the input channel, 10th May, 1962.

Left: The single tipping wagon at Billing. The only time I looked inside it was loaded with a mixture of stones, corks and condoms. 4th June, 1966

Sewage Works, Finedon

According to *Pocket Book D* Kettering Borough Council in Northfield Road (SP862798) had an early standard gauge petrol locomotive and a 2 ft gauge one as well, both worth making a detour to see when making for another visit to the Furnaces railway on 30th April, 1962. The standard gauge locomotive was in its shed, but there was no sign of the narrow gauge one in the yard until my guide took me to a tarpaulin covered object (*upper*). Removing the covers (*lower*) revealed No. 20, F.Hibberd 1669 of 1930, once used at Finedon sewage works. Note engine controls and the klaxon horn on the cab front.

Sewage Works, Wollaston

Three miles south of Wellingborough, Wollaston Parish Council operated a small sewage works (SP898630), which had a monorail to serve the drying beds. The sole locomotive and wagon was a Mark 2 Road Machines unit, having hydraulic drive to both axles, and a seat for the driver (*upper:* photographed 3rd May, 1964). Two tracks served the drying beds, with a siding to the brick engine shed. (*lower*). Near the road were concrete bays (*facing page*) for loading lorries or storing dry sludge (used as fertilizer) before despatch.

Loading bays. Note the way rails have been disconnected, a simple operation, to form points.

Sewage Works, Roade

I was told there was a similar system at nearby Doddington, which I never tried to find, but there was another system in a sewage works just south of Roade station (SP758513) which I first saw from a passing train. If Wollaston was any guide, it was probably operated by Roade Parish Council. Two tracks served the settling tanks then the monorail climbed to what I noted as drying beds. The unit, assumed to be a standard Road Machine product, was housed in a creosoted wooden shed. My visit here made a change – usually if I went to Roade it was to watch expresses on the main line, hauled by Duchesses and Royal Scots!

Settling tanks in right distance, wooden shed in centre beyond sloping line to drying beds near works entrance on left, 29th August, 1964.

Timber Yard, Cotton End Northampton

Trenery & Sons Ltd, Cotton End, close to the River Nene in Bridge Street, Northampton, (SP 754596) laid an 18 in. gauge hand-operated system within their timber yard in the early 1900s. Since the Second World War it had been disused, and much of the track concreted over, but five out of about a dozen small wooden trolleys to carry timber remained in 1965. They were 60 in. long, 27¾ in. wide, with 8½ in. diameter wheels loose on their axles set at 23½ in. wheelbase. The frames were 6¾ x 2¾ in. wood. Both photographs 11th September, 1965.

Examples of the original wooden trolleys used on the system.

Some remaining visible track, with the ex-RAF bomb trolleys (assumed) then used to carry timber within the yard.